Fun with Bible Friends

ISBN 0-7847-2025-8

14 13 12 11 10 09 08 07   7 6 5 4 3 2 1

Standard®
PUBLISHING
Bringing The Word to Life

Cincinnati, Ohio

Animals boarded Noah's ark.

"They went into the boat in groups of two." *Genesis 7:9*

Joseph's father gave him a colorful coat.

Baby Moses was safe in his basket boat.

Joshua obeyed God.

"Now, shout! The Lord has given you this city." *Joshua 6:16*

David praised God with songs on his harp.

God kept Daniel safe in the lions' den.

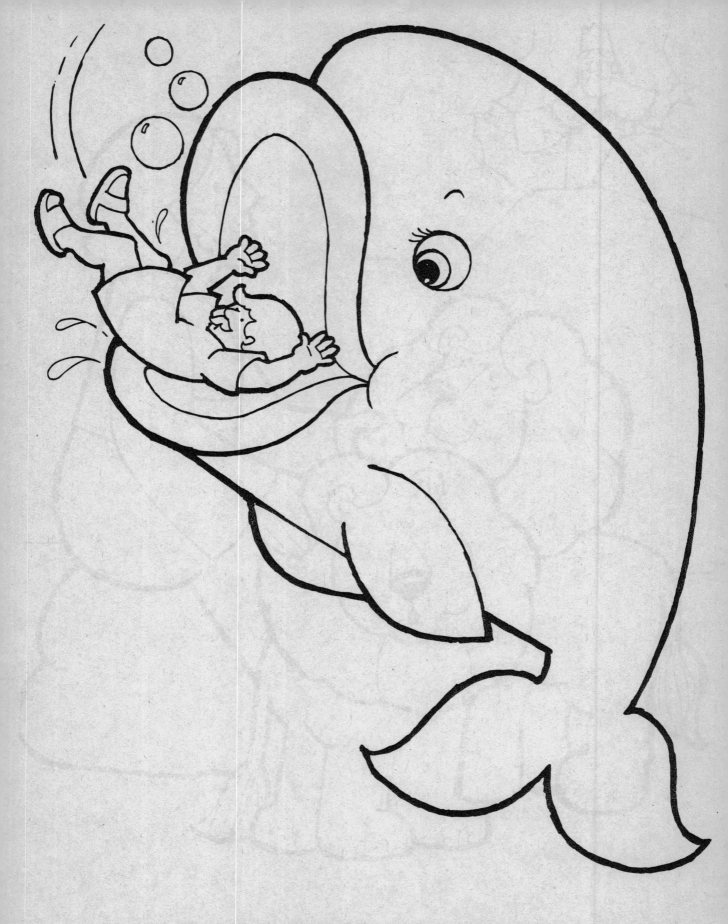

God sent a big fish to swallow Jonah.

Esther spoke bravely to the king.

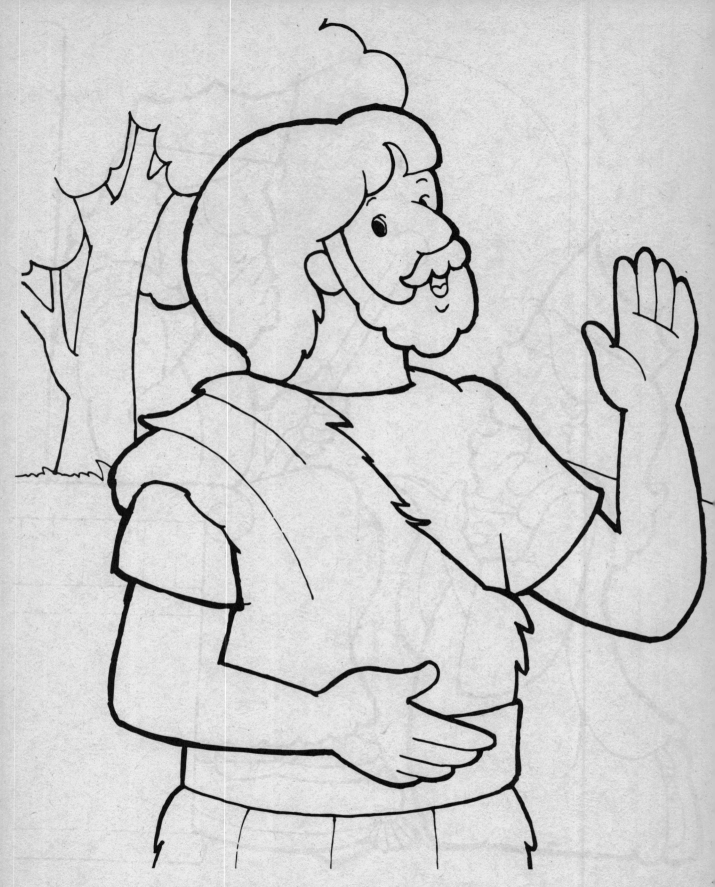

John the Baptist had a message for people.
"Prepare the way for the Lord." *Luke 3:4*

Baby Jesus was born in Bethlehem.

Jesus stopped a storm on the sea.

A small boy shared his lunch with Jesus.

Zacchaeus climbed a tree to see Jesus.

Timothy's mother and grandmother taught him about God.

"Let the little children come to me." *Mark 10:14*